God's Plan Just For You!

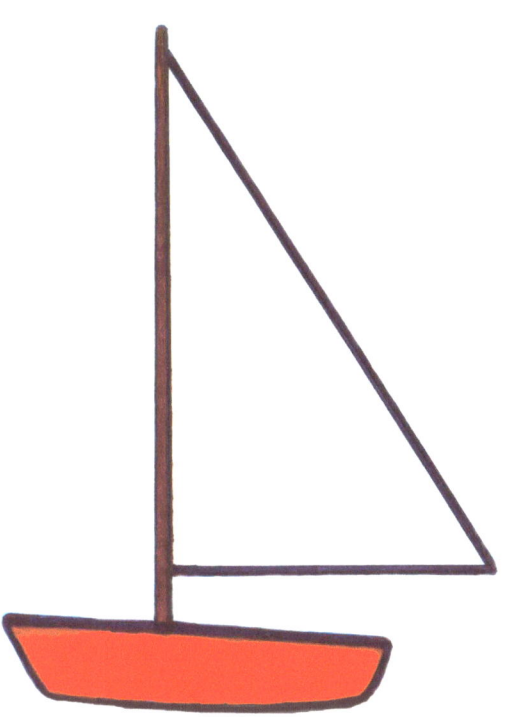

by Beto Peña

illustrations by Neva Harrison

God's Plan Just for You!

Story copyright © 2016 by Beto Peña
Illustrations copyright © 2016 by Neva Harrison
All rights reserved. Published by Beto Peña
ISBN-13: 978-0-9909980-1-3   ISBN-10: 0-9909980-1-0

For Evan, my son.

*Thank you to my princess, Gina, and to all of you who offered invaluable input.

Scripture quotations marked (GW) are taken from GOD'S WORD®, © 1995 God's Word to the Nations. Used by permission of Baker Publishing Group.

Scripture quotations marked (NIrV) are taken from the Holy Bible, New International Reader's Version®, NIrV® Copyright © 1995, 1996, 1998, 2014 by Biblica, Inc.™ Used by permission of Zondervan. All rights reserved worldwide. www.zondervan.com The "NIrV" and "New International Reader's Version" are trademarks registered in the United States Patent and Trademark Office by Biblica, Inc.™

Scriptures quotations marked (NCV) taken from the New Century Version®. Copyright © 2005 by Thomas Nelson. Used by permission. All rights reserved.

Scripture quotations marked (NLT) are taken from the Holy Bible, New Living Translation, copyright ©1996, 2004, 2007, 2013, 2015 by Tyndale House Foundation. Used by permission of Tyndale House Publishers, Inc., Carol Stream, Illinois 60188. All rights reserved.

No part of this publication may be reproduced, stored in a retrieval system, or transmitted in any form or by any means, electronic, mechanical, photocopying, recording, or otherwise, without written permission of the author. For information regarding permission, please visit www.DesignedToBeYou.com.

How did this book happen?

It's a Sunday morning, 3:30 AM and I am sleeping soundly! Suddenly, I feel prompted to get out of bed because God seemed to be impressing on me a brand new sermon to preach in just a few hours! I'm not sure He realized that I already had one prepared! (that was humor) In just a few minutes, He had given me a complete message called, "Designed to Be You," which shared how each of us were uniquely created and gifted by God to bring Him glory as we serve others. **God's Plan Just for You!** is an adaptation of that message intended for preschoolers.

This book may be read in story form by following the left pages, while the right hand pages are the complementing scripture references upon which the story is based.

Did you know God created you in a very special way? It's true!

Put on your new nature, created
to be like God -
truly righteous and holy.

Ephesians 4:24 (NLT)

God loves you sooooo much, He made only one You!

I will give thanks to You because I have been so amazingly and miraculously made.

Psalm 139:14 (GW)

He gave you arms and legs and itty-bitty toes...

God put each part of the body together as He wanted.

1 Corinthians 12:18 (GW)

Eyes and ears and a cute little nose!

*...we are God's masterpiece.
He has created us new
in Christ Jesus...*

Ephesians 2:10a (NLT)

What is all this for?

Like boats are made to sail on the sea,

God had a plan when He made you and me.

We are God's masterpiece.
He has created us new in Christ
Jesus, so we can do the good
things He planned for us
long ago.

Ephesians 2:10 (NLT)

We are made to Love God and His people too,

this is what we are created to do.

Love the Lord your God with all your heart and all your soul... Love your neighbor as yourself.

Matthew 22:37,39 (NIRV)

How do we love God?

By reading the Bible, obeying His word, and talking to God, our voices are heard!

If you love Me, you will obey
My commandments.

John 14:15 (GW)

How do we love people?

God gave us all special gifts we can use,
to help other people and spread His good news!

Those who believe in God will be careful to use their lives for doing good. These things are good and will help everyone.

Titus 3:8b (NCV)

He alone decides which gift each person should have...

1 Corinthians 12:11b (NLT)

What can you do well?

Can you draw a picture?... Help clean up a mess?

Give clothes or toys to those who have less?

God has given us different gifts for doing certain things well.

Romans 12:6a (NLT)

Serving somebody with a smile on our face,
is a great way to show them a bit of God's grace!

*God's gifts of grace come
in many forms.
Each of you has received a gift
in order to serve others.
You should use it faithfully.*

1 Peter 4:10 (NIRV)

As we help people, they see God's love,
'cause all of our kindness comes from above!

Let your light shine in front
of people. Then they will see the
good that you do and praise
your Father in Heaven.

Matthew 5:16 (GW)

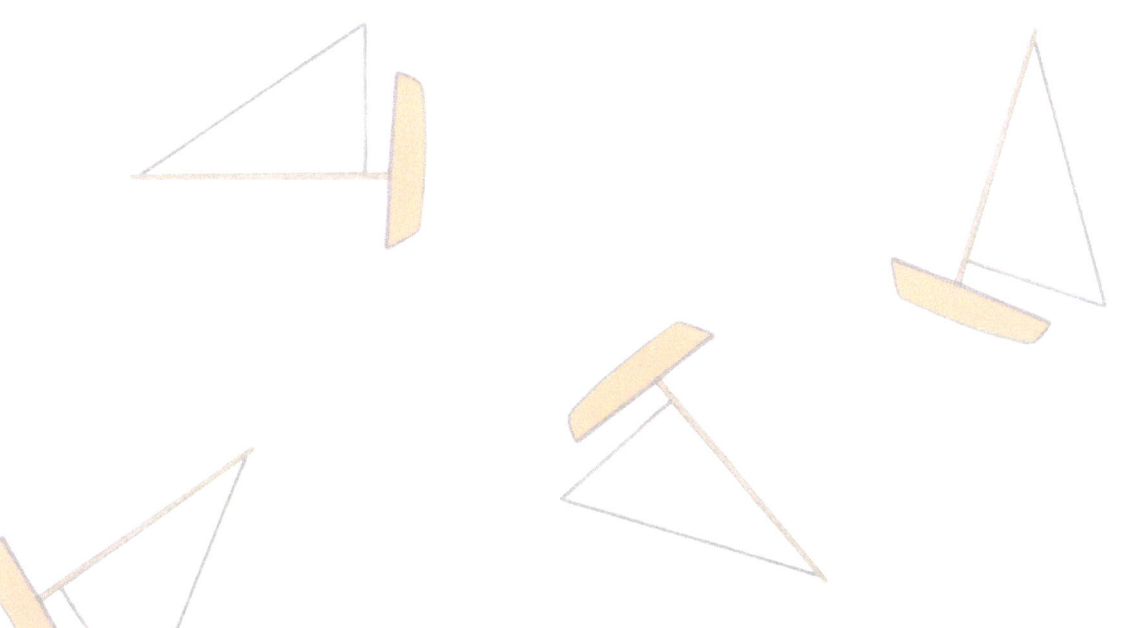

God's Plan Just for You!
creators

Beto has been involved in ministry since 2001, serving most of those years as a children's pastor, and has a knack for relating to kids on their level. Having a Master's Degree in Counseling, his passion lies in helping others discover who they are in Christ, what their God-given purpose is, and how to live out that purpose daily.
Beto currently lives in Boerne, Texas with his wife and son.

Born in California in 1948, Neva discovered her passion for art at the age of 5. Travels through the Western states and a sense of wonder drove her to develop her self-taught, God-given gift with excitement and adventure. Though having done commission work for 40 years, she leans more towards creating from her imagination and plans on painting and enjoying life with all it's beauty until the end.

www.ingramcontent.com/pod-product-compliance
Lightning Source LLC
Chambersburg PA
CBHW041540040426
42446CB00002B/179